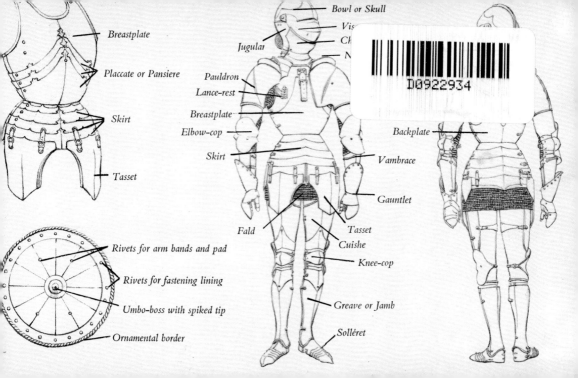

Breastplate

Placcate or Pansiere

Skirt

Tasset

Rivets for arm bands and pad

Rivets for fastening lining

Umbo-boss with spiked tip

Ornamental border

Bowl or Skull

Vis...

Ch...

N...

Jugular

Pauldron

Lance-rest

Breastplate

Elbow-cop

Skirt

Fald

Tasset

Cuishe

Knee-cop

Greave or Jamb

Solléret

Vambrace

Gauntlet

Backplate

ABOUT THE COVER:

The Earl of Cumberland was Queen Elizabeth's personal champion, and his armor was embellished with a design in which were included the Tudor rose, the lover's knot, the fleur-de-lis, and Elizabeth's initial.

CREDITS AND ACKNOWLEDGMENTS: *The Metropolitan Museum of Art has generously given permission to illustrate drawings from development charts and the following objects: Bashford Dean Memorial Collection, 13 (center and right), 14, 15, 22–23 (knight's armor) 36; Dick Fund, 17 (left and right), 25 (E), 32 (shield), 43 (flintlock pistol); Gift of Helen Fahnestock Hubbard, 1929, in memory of her father, Harris C. Fahnestock, 13 (left); Gift of J. Pierpont Morgan, 19; Munsey Bequest, 16; Pulitzer Fund, 18; Gift of William H. Riggs, 10–11, 37 (right), 43 (top two pistols); Rogers Fund, 12, 17 (center), 18, 22–23 (horse armor), 25 (D), 27 (center); Gift of Alan Rutherfurd Stuyvesant, 27 (left): Whittelsey Fund, 21.*

Pierpont Morgan Library, 6; Canterbury Cathedral, 8–9; Historical Museum, Berne, 20; Tower Armouries, London, 26; Waffensammlung, Kunsthistorisches Museum, Vienna, 27 (right), 35, 38 (lower right); National Gallery, Washington, D.C., 33; Art Reference Bureau—Pinakothek, Munich, 34. From the author's collection and library: helmet, 25 (C), 28–30, 31 (right), 32 (left), 36, 38 (except lower right), 39–40, 42, 43 (bottom). Except for page 34, all photographs are from Francis G. Mayer.

ARMS AND ARMOR

BY STEPHEN V. GRANCSAY

CURATOR EMERITUS

DEPARTMENT OF ARMS AND ARMOR

THE METROPOLITAN MUSEUM OF ART, NEW YORK

THE ODYSSEY PRESS · NEW YORK

"ARMS AND THE MAN I SING," said Virgil at the start of his *Aeneid*, and, indeed, men have often glorified the arms of a hero as well as the hero himself. ■ When Homer told of the Greek assault on Troy, he wrote of "the warriors in their garb of battle — resplendent helmets, bossed shields, plated cuirasses, and ashen spears. The glory of their arms lit up the sky; the glitter of bronze rippled like laughter over the plain . . ." ■ In other ages, other men—poets, princes, and the warriors themselves—felt the grandeur and

David, king of Israel, slaying Shobach, a Syrian captain. From a mid-13th century book of Old Testament illustrations, the armor and weapons shown—mail, flat-topped helms, shields, swords and lances—are of that period.

power that clung to the arms that made a man a hero. Kings paid fortunes to clothe themselves from head to foot in glistening metal. Artists gave to the designs for decorated helmets and shields the same care that they gave to a painting for a cathedral. The consecrated arms of a knight were stored, not in an armory, but in a church. And, when armor passed from father to son, it carried with it a tradition and a responsibility. ■ Certain basic types of armor have been worn throughout the ages. Soft armor, a protective coat of quilted fabric, is the most ancient. It came to Europe from the East —the *acton,* a padded undergarment worn beneath metal armor in the Middle Ages, took its name from the Arabic *al qutun,* from which

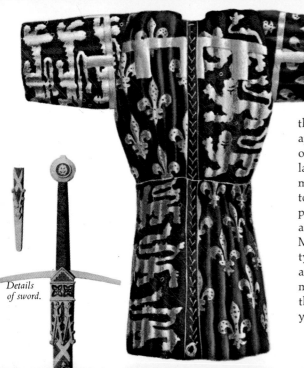

Details of sword.

the word "cotton" is also derived. Metal armor appeared at least forty centuries ago. It was of copper or bronze in the form of scale or lamellar armor and mail. The scale armor was made by sewing or riveting small metal scales to a backing of cloth. In lamellar armor, this process was improved; the scales were pierced along the edges and laced together with thongs. Mail, more difficult to construct than the other types and consequently more expensive, was a mesh of individually riveted, hand-formed metal links, sometimes as many as a hundred thousand in a single shirt. ■ For thousands of years, these basic types of armor in many varia-

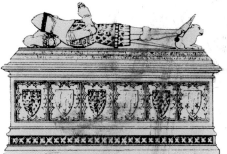

The effigy of the Black Prince (left) is of copper gilt with enamel enrichments. Plate armor encloses the limbs. The details at left, along with those at lower left on the opposite page, are from the effigy. From top to bottom they are a detail of the sword belt; a detail of the part of the helm to which was also attached the mail protecting the face, neck, and shoulders; and the sword hilt and scabbard. The two shields display the fleur-de-lis of France and the lions of England and the three feathers of the Prince of Wales.

9

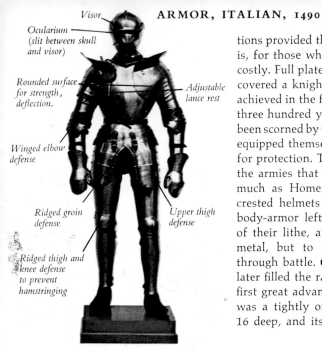

Visor

Ocularium
(slit between skull
and visor)

Rounded surface
for strength,
deflection.

Adjustable
lance rest

Winged elbow
defense

Ridged groin
defense

Upper thigh
defense

Ridged thigh and
knee defense
to prevent
hamstringing

tions provided the protection for the armies of the world—that is, for those who could afford armor, for it has always been costly. Full plate armor, the sheath of jointed metal units that covered a knight from head to foot, was a late development, achieved in the fourteenth century and perfected over the next three hundred years. Such over-all armor-plating would have been scorned by the early warriors, the Greeks, for instance, who equipped themselves first for speed and mobility, and second for protection. The hoplites, the heavy-armed foot soldiers of the armies that saved Greece from the Persians, were armed much as Homer said his heroes were. They wore strong, crested helmets and carried heavy round shields, but their body-armor left their thighs and abdomens exposed. Proud of their lithe, athletic bodies, they trusted, not to plates of metal, but to skill and endurance to carry them safely through battle. ■ It was these spirited Hellenic warriors who later filled the ranks of the Macedonian phalanx, the world's first great advance in organized fighting power. The phalanx was a tightly ordered battering-ram of men, 16 across and 16 deep, and its primary weapon was a 21-foot pike. Alexander the Great put it to use to help him conquer the ancient world. ■ The Romans devised an even better military system based on the more maneuverable legion—and they conquered an even larger empire. The legionary's armor, of course, had to be suited to long marches and active movement. For the men of the lines, there were jackets of hide and iron headpieces; officers added corselets and shoulder defenses formed of iron bands. This heavy infantry relied on an extensive system of supply bases which eventually proved vulnerable to cavalry raids. The first of the deadly light cavalry appeared among the Balkan Goths. Following them through the everwidening cracks in the frontier defenses of the Roman Empire came the barbaric hordes. Little is known of the barbarians' arms or armor, but the warriors themselves were fierce rovers who fought like demons. They broke the empire into pieces, conquered the fragments, and sent Europe into chaos. When the dust cleared, the first of the knights of chivalry had appeared to try to set things in order. ■ In 1066, at the time of the Norman conquest of England, the new knights wore iron helmets, a complete armor of mail, and carried a great

Keel ridge
for strength

Mail secured
to helmet base

Separate
shoulder piece

Mail hauberk
for movement
in saddle.

Greaves
shaped to leg.

Hinged shin
and calf plates

Holes for
mail shoes

kite-shaped shield. Through the years, the shield became smaller. In the thirteenth century it shrank into a triangle; by 1300 it was so small that it could no longer be used to carry a wounded knight or to bear a corpse. The body armor also began to change. Mail was comfortable enough and certainly it allowed great freedom of movement (young esquires accustomed themselves to the weight of their new suits of mail by turning somersaults in them). However, against the crushing and bruising blows of a mace, mail was a painfully inadequate defense. The armorers began to add on steel plates, piece by piece, as reinforcement. The first plates were provided for the knees, particularly vulnerable spots on a mounted man. By the time of the Battle of Crécy, in 1346, there were suits made up entirely of plates. ■ The construction of a workable metal skin for a man was a challenge that

12

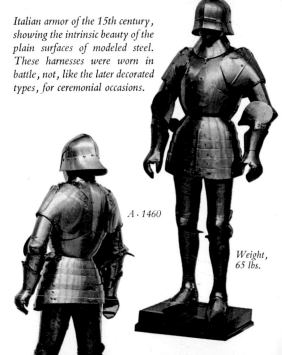

Italian armor of the 15th century, showing the intrinsic beauty of the plain surfaces of modeled steel. These harnesses were worn in battle, not, like the later decorated types, for ceremonial occasions.

A · 1460

Weight, 65 lbs.

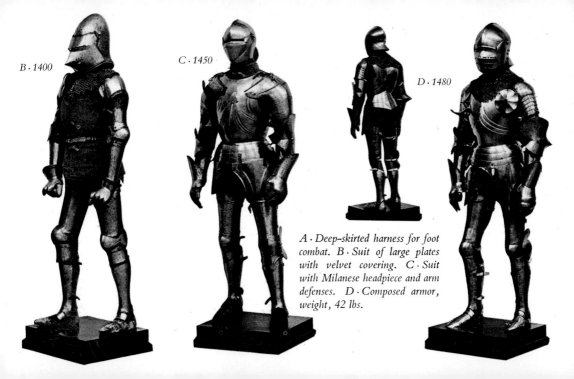

B · 1400

C · 1450

D · 1480

A · Deep-skirted harness for foot combat. B · Suit of large plates with velvet covering. C · Suit with Milanese headpiece and arm defenses. D · Composed armor, weight, 42 lbs.

Landsknecht officer, 1545.

fired the imaginations of craftsmen and engineers, and, in the armor of the Middle Ages and Renaissance, the designing of contours in steel attained a perfection that has not since been surpassed. To make armor that would protect a warrior and yet not hinder his movements, the armorer needed a sculptor's understanding of human anatomy. He had to know the play of every muscle, the hinging of every joint—both human and in metal. Never has the kinship between artist and engineer been more apparent than in a "hollow sculpture" of steel, the work of a fifteenth or sixteenth century armorer. The steel itself is light, strong, and beautiful. Its contours follow those of the figure it was designed to protect: It is never lifeless; it has equilibrium and a certain vibrant grace—its posture is good. ■ To acquire such armor, a knight was willing to pay a high price and to travel far, to one of the towns that grew famous for the skill of their armorers. In the fifteenth and sixteenth centuries, the greatest center of armor-making in Europe was Milan. It was said that the craftsmen along the city's Street of the Armorers could outfit an army in a few days, and it is a fact that they armed the kings of France and Spain, the dukes of Italy, and more than once the cavalry of opposing countries. To the ablest Milanese armorers, the Missaglia and Negroli, came renown, fortune, and royal commissions. Tomasso Missaglia was knighted by the Duke Filippo Maria Visconti in 1435; fifteen years later, Francesco Sforza, the leader of a new regime, excused him from paying taxes. In 1491, the armorers of Milan celebrated the wedding of Lodovico Sforza by lining their street with effigies of mounted warriors clad entirely with mail and damascened

Emperor Maximilian I in fluted armor.

Armor of the Earl of Cumberland, made between 1590 and 1595. The best-preserved Elizabethan armor we have; one of the few showing original colors.

steel. It was a magnificent display of the product which salesmen from Milan sold in every court in Europe. As it happened, they also sold colored trappings and ribbons. A man from Milan was called a "Milaner," a word which survives in English today as "milliner." ■ The city of Augsburg was Milan's greatest rival in the art of constructing fine armor. Augsburg's fame was established by the family of Helmschmied, whose name meant "helmet-maker." And it was Desiderius Helmschmied who once decorated a shield with the representation of a bull charging a Roman soldier whose armor bore the word "Negrol"—a jibe at the Negroli, the Helmschmied's Milanese competitors. In producing their masterpieces of shaped and engraved metal, the Helmschmieds collaborated with some of the finest artists of their time. Among them were Hans Burgkmair the Elder and Albrecht Dürer. Both artists worked for

16th CENTURY ARMOR

BELOW AND RIGHT: *Armor of Henry Herbert, 2nd Earl of Pembroke. English, 1575–80.*

LEFT: *Parade armor of Henry II of France. French, 1550.*

RIGHT: *Armor of Anne de Montmorency, Constable of France. French, 1555.*

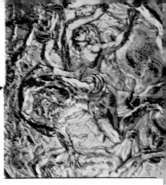

Parade helmet, probably made for Cosimo de' Medici or Henry II of France by a French or Italian armorer in 1550. It is embossed in low relief with the battle of centaurs and Lapiths, gorgons, and a Greek wave pattern on the crest. It appears in a portrait of Ferdinand I de' Medici in the Pitti Palace and in one of his son in the Metropolitan.

the Emperor Maximilian I and, as a part of their duties, they designed and decorated his armor. ■ For every knight, acquiring a suit of armor was a matter of custom tailoring. The fit of the suits was most important, and those that still exist display a surprising range of sizes. There are many harnesses that were made for men six feet tall, and some that were fashioned for children who were destined to be knights. In the Tower Armouries in London a series of suits presents a unique and revealing portrait of Henry VIII. The shape of the king as a young man is preserved in a suit of armor for fighting on foot; the waist measures a princely 35". But after years of good living one of his harnesses has a girth of 38"; a much later one has a regal 54" waistline. ■ Most men of war did not attain such kingly proportions. The study of their armor shows that the typical knight was a brawny, muscular man, whose body

Casque made by Philip de Negroli in 1543, probably for Francis I of France. The boldness of the embossing and the bronze-black patina give the helmet the appearance of having been cast. Actually it was sculpted in cold steel.

reflected his activities and way of life. He had broad shoulders and the slender legs of a modern jockey, because he did little walking but went to exercise, as he did to battle, on horseback. In the Middle Ages, war depended on horse flesh. A country that possessed few horses had little hope of winning wars, and a man who possessed no horse was not a knight—he was not, in fact, a gentleman. This rule of society was so universally accepted that the very words that mean gentleman—*chevalier* in French, *cavalliere* in Italian, *caballero* in Spanish, and *Ritter* in German—all originally meant only "rider on a horse." For a knight of chivalry, no skill was more important than fine horsemanship, and hard riding, combined with the use of arms and armor, required the utmost strength and dexterity. In *Henry V*, the young king, a marvel among warriors but a tongue-tied wooer, tells Katherine that he would win her easily enough if he could woo a lady "by vaulting into my saddle with my armor on my back." ■ The knights did not, of

LEFT: *A 15th century French tapestry showing Julius Caesar crossing the Rubicon (far left) and his victory over Pompey at Pharsalia.* RIGHT: *Knights in armor fighting wild bears. The bears could not grasp the slippery armor.*

course, spend day after day in suits of plate armor. Even in battle they sometimes preferred to wear the more flexible shirts of mail. Mail could also be useful in emergencies—it was kept in a saddle-bag and donned in a hurry if the knight ran into trouble in town or along the road. Another popular defense, one which had the added advantage that it looked elegant in town, was the brigandine. Literally, the word meant "armor for brigands," or foot soldiers. It was a jacket of velvet or other rich material with an interlining of row upon row of small overlapping plates secured by exposed rivets. It could be worn without much discomfort, though Benvenuto Cellini said that gentlemen often had their town jackets of cloth cut and decorated with studs to look like brigandines and trusted that their enemies would not dare

LEFT AND RIGHT: *Armor for man and horse, German, 1548, the work of Kunz Lochner of Nuremberg.*

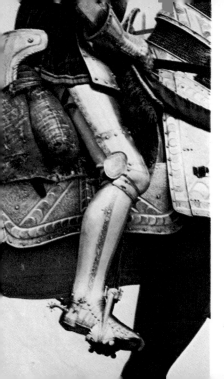

The embossed letters on the horse's chest armor translate as "I trust in God with all my heart, Johann Ernst, Duke of Saxony." The detail at left shows the beautifully-fashioned stirrup and a spur. Spurs were the symbols of knighthood and were buried with their owner. Stirrups were an Asiatic invention; the date of their introduction in Europe is uncertain. They were unknown to the Greeks and Romans.

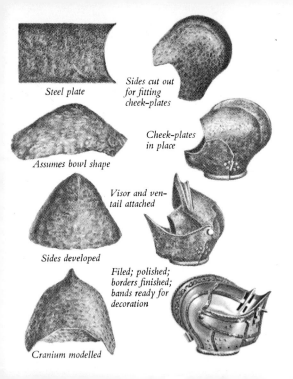

Steel plate

Sides cut out for fitting cheek-plates

Assumes bowl shape

Cheek-plates in place

Visor and ventail attached

Sides developed

Filed; polished; borders finished; bands ready for decoration

Cranium modelled

to investigate too closely. Cellini also noted that Roman dandies had taken to wearing shirts of mail, not for protection, but to impress the ladies. ■ It was not surprising that the styles and decoration of armor and civil dress should influence each other, especially in an age in which the design of clothes was so important that artists like Leonardo and Raphael gave it their attention. After all, chivalric armor had begun as a metal version of a woolen gown, and armor, however fully it covered the body, was always worn with trappings of cloth. From about the middle of the thirteenth century, a surcoat bearing heraldic arms was usually worn over the suit of mail. The emblem identified the knight and often saved his life, for it informed

Some of the steps in making a helmet. The bowl is hammered out of a single piece of steel. The parts are filed, polished, etched, fire-gilt, finished, and then assembled.

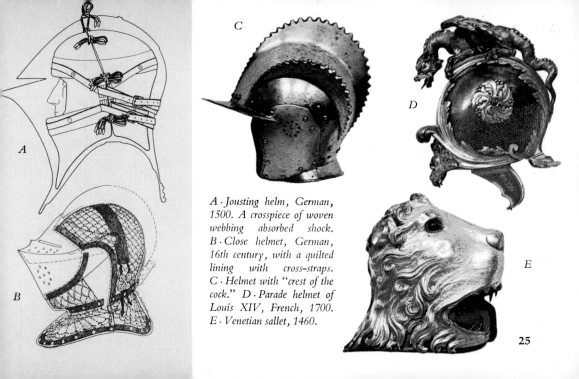

A · Jousting helm, German, 1500. A crosspiece of woven webbing absorbed shock. B · Close helmet, German, 16th century, with a quilted lining with cross-straps. C · Helmet with "crest of the cock." D · Parade helmet of Louis XIV, French, 1700. E · Venetian sallet, 1460.

25

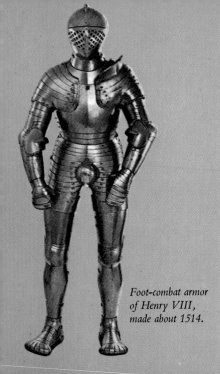

Foot-combat armor of Henry VIII, made about 1514.

his enemies that he was of a rank that could afford to pay ransom. Kings and military leaders, whose presence on the field greatly influenced the morale of their soldiers, soon recognized the usefulness of emblems, plumes, and crests which made their identity unmistakable. William the Conqueror, who lived before such trappings came into use, had to lift his conical nasal helmet before he could convince his men at Hastings, in 1066, that he still lived. The later medieval kings had a different sort of problem—they were so well marked that it was necessary to mislead the enemy by sending several men onto the field dressed exactly as they were. Thus Shakespeare's *Richard III* could exclaim, "I think there be six Richmonds in the field. Five I have slain today instead of him." ■ On state occasions and at tournaments, knights and kings alike appeared in the rich armor that their artists so often painted and their poets described with such delight—armor that was colored, gilded, covered with embroidered materials, and decorated with monumental crests, jeweled crowns, and fluttering ribbons. No hero of any age ever surpassed the magnificence of a medieval knight when he entered the lists to display his prowess. Even his horse

16th CENTURY ARMOR

BELOW AND RIGHT: *Armor of Galiot de Genouilhac, French or Italian, dated 1527.*

ABOVE AND LEFT: *Maximilian armor, named for the Emperor. German, about 1505.*

RIGHT: *Parade armor of King Maximilian II of Bohemia, dated 1549.*

was enveloped in brilliant trappings. ■ These military games were the most important of the sports that kept the knight in training for war. The tournament was a contest of skill in which several mounted combatants, divided into two teams, engaged in battle like two opposing armies. The joust was a competition for two adversaries, who opposed each other with blunted lances, or sometimes with the sharp weapons of genuine combat. Everything about the games was attended by much chivalrous ceremony. Before the combats, the squires carried their masters' crested helms to the hall, where the king-at-arms judged each blazon and where visitors—especially ladies—examined them with a critical eye. The display of helms also provided an opportunity for expelling from the tournament any entrant whose blazon identified him as a man guilty of an act unworthy of a knight. ■ The shield, like the helmet, had its

28

ABOVE: *Jousting, from the tourney book of Duke William IV of Bavaria. The book begins in 1510 and exhibits eight separate forms of the tourney.*

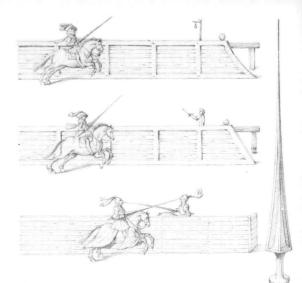

RIGHT: *from* De Pluvinal, *1625. Knights practiced for the joust by (top) running, or tilting, at the ring; (center) running at a quintain; and (bottom) running at each other.*

When fairly hit, the ring became detached and remained on the head of the lance. The quintain was an object to be tilted at, in this case fashioned as a Turk.

ceremonial significance, but it was the sword that was held in greatest honor as the symbol of the virtues of a warrior. Christian and heathen fighting men both honored the sword. It was the emblem of independence. Its surrender was a token of defeat and submission. The touch of its blade on the shoulder of the neophyte initiated him into the company of knights. Nothing was too good for the sword; the most precious materials were used to decorate it and the finest artists worked on it. ■ The sword which a medieval knight carried into battle had a straight, two-edged blade and a simple hilt—the knight relied on his gauntlet to protect his hand. The blade of the sword was stout, for a combat of knights was a rugged contest of crushing blows in which a man's superiority depended on the quality of his armor and his ability to deal heavier blows than his opponent. ■ From the beginning, the sword

FAR LEFT: *The exhibition of helms before the tournament, from Grünenberg's* Wappenbuch *(Munich, 1483).* ABOVE: *Drawings in water color of tilters, from a sixteenth century tournament book.* RIGHT: *Jousting armor of the type known as Stechzeug. Figures A, B, and C are details of the lance; C is the vamplate. Figure D shows the front of the jousting armor; it was heavy, the helms alone often weighed twenty pounds. No leg armor was worn. Figure H is a back view of Figure D. Figure F is the shield which was tied to the left side of the breastplate to present a glancing surface. Figure G shows the lining of the helmet. Figure E is another upper harness.*

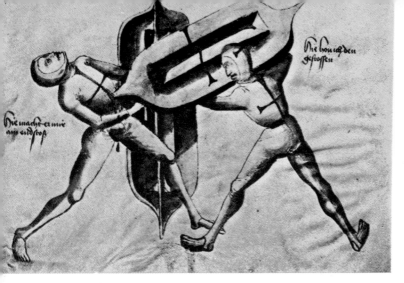

Shield
Hungarian-type
15th century

Combat with shields. Entitled "He gives me the final blow," this is an illustration from Hans Talhofer's Fencing Book *of the year 1467. Talhofer's was the standard treatise on pole-axe and sword play and skill-at-arms.*

and armor made of fine metal were the equipment of kings and the members of the nobility, the symbols of the division between knight and commoner, between cavalry and infantry. In feudal times, the possession of arms and armor made one man the master of many, for the commoners at first had almost no effective weapons and no means of acquiring them. A knight on an armored horse could quickly trample down the foot soldiers. However, with the development of archery, the system began to change. In 1346, the English yeomen came to the Battle of Crécy armed with the longbow, a weapon which the knights soon learned to respect. The old crossbow, known from Roman times, had always been a formidable weapon; its heavy bolts, which were fired from a bow bent by a windlass or lever, pierced all but the heaviest armor. But it took time to load and bend a crossbow. A man with a longbow could shoot quickly —five or six arrows to each bolt from a crossbow—and his effective range was at least a hundred yards. The arrows could not penetrate good armor, but they were most effective against

Shield with painting of the youthful David, by Andrea del Castagno. Some of the most distinguished masters, including Leonardo da Vinci, painted shields.

horses, which were maddened by the slightest wound and could not be controlled. It was an unpleasant experience for a knight in armor to be thrown from a horse. ■ In 1487 Maximilian I armed his infantry, the Landsknecht, with another weapon that was effective against cavalry. This was the halberd, a lance-like weapon which could be used to cut as well as to thrust. Its hook or beak could drag a knight from his saddle or trip his horse; its spike could perforate mail. ■ Polearms, maces, and war hammers were developed from the farm tools that once had been the only arms of the peasants called to the service of their feudal lords. The mace

Detail from "The Martyrdom of St. Sebastian," an altarpiece by Hans Holbein the Elder, about 1515. The crossbow was bent with a windlass, a lever, or a cranequin. The cranequin is an instrument that works on the same principle as a lifting jack. The bolt pierced all but very heavy armor.

was simply a heavy staff or club. It was made either wholly or in part of metal and was capable of breaking through armor. The war hammer, as its name suggests, was a very heavy hammer. It usually had one blunt and one pointed extremity. The war hammers used by the infantry against knights in armor had long handles. This weapon, too, could break through armor. The polearm could count among its ancestors one weapon, the spear, and three humbler implements, the axe, the reaping hook, and the scythe. By the sixteenth century, however, the polearm had been raised to the nobility; it was an object of ceremonial use, it bore heraldic arms, and often it was sumptuously decorated. ■ As the foot soldiers' weapons improved, the knights increased the weight of their armor, lost their mobility, and became more vulnerable than ever. The problem of armor-breaking ceased to be the most important one in a fight,

A crossbowman in the service of the Emperor Maximilian I, German, early 16th century. The crossbow was the favorite European military weapon from 1200 to 1460.

and soldiers who were accustomed to using the sword without wearing armor developed skill in fencing. The Italians were the first to perceive that the point of the sword was, in fencing, superior to the edge. They accordingly produced a lighter weapon by reducing the width of the blade and by narrowing the hilt. They gradually developed the cunning swordplay known as rapier fence. The late sixteenth century swept hilt, with its gracefully branching guards, was the culmination of a hundred years of development. After 1650 the sword degenerated as a weapon of warfare, but it remained in use as a dress or court sword. No longer the arm of the rank and file of infantry, it became once more the emblem of the gentleman, a sign of

Mounted knight accompanied by a Landsknecht, German, 1545. The Landsknecht carried halberds, a more effective weapon than the lance carried by the knight. Armed with a halberd, the foot soldier had little to fear.

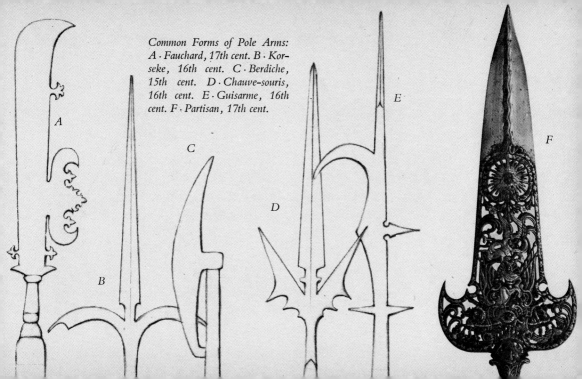

Common Forms of Pole Arms:
A · Fauchard, 17th cent. B · Korseke, 16th cent. C · Berdiche, 15th cent. D · Chauve-souris, 16th cent. E · Guisarme, 16th cent. F · Partisan, 17th cent.

A

B

C

D

E

F

ABOVE: *Fencing with sword and dagger. The figure at right is delivering a time thrust (an attack delivered between two movements of the adversary's attack) under his opponent's blade after the latter has lunged with both hands high. The illustration is from* La Scherma (1640) *by Francesco Alfieri, the master of the Fencing Academy at Padua. By Alfieri's time, the dimensions of the sword had been reduced by a few inches and its weight by many ounces.*

38

rank. Training in the use of the sword was an essential part of a gentleman's education now, and he was expected always to be ready to draw it. After 1780, however, dueling with swords went out of favor, and affairs of honor were settled with the pistol. ■ The first guns were cannon, which appeared about 1300. Then, around 1460, handguns began to supersede the crossbow on the battlefields of Europe. The English infantrymen kept their famed longbows throughout most of the sixteenth century. Indeed, in the seventeenth century, English pikemen were sometimes armed with bows in order to return the enemy's musket fire. At the time of the American Revolution, when the Continental Army had difficulty finding ammunition, Benjamin Franklin remembered the longbows and thought that perhaps, with their rapid fire, they might be put to use against the British flintlocks. Apparently

ABOVE LEFT: *Sword and cloak. Parries with the cloak were practically the same as with the dagger. The adversary's sword-arm was rendered useless by throwing the cloak over his blade. Left: Dress rapier with solid gold hilt. The workmanship is unusually intricate and beautiful. Right: Fencing with the two-hand sword. From Albrecht Dürer's* Fencing Book, *German, 1512.*

it had not occurred to Franklin that the cost and trouble of making arrows had had more than a little to do with the discarding of the bows. ■ John Adams had more up-to-date ideas. From Philadelphia he wrote about "a peculiar kind of musket, called a rifle"—the Pennsylvania rifle. Sporting rifles had been known since the fifteenth century. However, no army could make extensive use of rifles until ways had been devised to produce them in large quantities with interchangeable parts. So the musket continued to be the weapon of the American forces until 1855. ■ The struggle between armor and missiles is endless. Medieval armor withstood the

normal impact of a heavy crossbow at short range. The first muskets did not make body armor obsolete; instead, they speeded up its development. The writings of military experts at the turn of the seventeenth century are filled with references to new armor that was high-proof, musket-proof, pistol-proof, and just plain proof. In the mid-seventeenth century, as musketry improved, it was not unusual for warriors to wear two breastplates, one over the other. The armorer was always ready to fashion protection that would resist musket and pistol shot, but he could do it only by using heavier and heavier plates. Military discipline required that this weighty and uncomfortable equipment be worn for hours at a stretch, and it was that which at last made the suits of steel obsolete. The men refused to wear them. English soldiers in the late sixteenth century reported for training and musters without their armor, and they

FROM LEFT: *A pikeman, a musketeer, and a caliver-man. The pike, made of ash, was about sixteen feet long. The musketeer had to handle so many accessories that he often held the bullet in his mouth. The caliver was a handgun lighter than the musket and was fired without a gunrest.*

demanded a penny a mile "over and besides the eight-pence a day for wages" before they would wear it on the march. Other soldiers set themselves against armor, wages or no. Some simply made certain that it got lost. ■ Today, however, body armor is in use again. The modern soldier has his "bullet-proof vest" and other forms of protection that have been developed to meet the requirements of the tactics of open warfare, the highly specialized duties of men in aircraft and in armored vehicles, and the increased use of high explosive ammunition instead of low-velocity shrapnel. The metal fragments from the explosive shell have an initial velocity greater than that of a bullet, but 80% of casualties in the air and on the ground

The foot soldier versus the cavalryman in armor. From J. J. Wallhausen's Art militaire a cheval, *Zutphen, 1621.* ABOVE: *pistol versus pistol.* BELOW: *lance versus musket.*

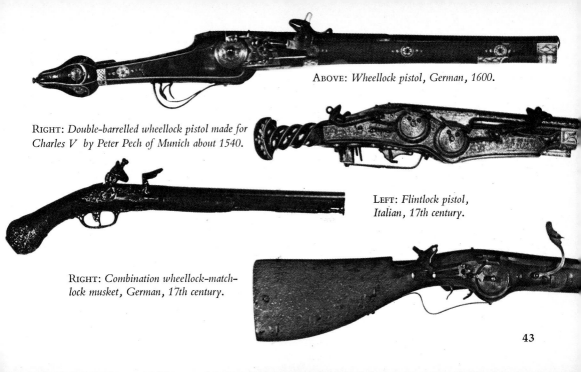

ABOVE: *Wheellock pistol, German, 1600.*

RIGHT: *Double-barrelled wheellock pistol made for Charles V by Peter Pech of Munich about 1540.*

LEFT: *Flintlock pistol, Italian, 17th century.*

RIGHT: *Combination wheellock-matchlock musket, German, 17th century.*

43

ABOVE: *Waist gunner wearing helmet and flak suit in action on a heavy bomber.* RIGHT: *infantryman wearing helmet and body armor.*

are caused by fragments of such shells traveling at comparatively low speeds. Light weight, modern body armor is designed to reduce these casualties to a minimum. It may not afford effective protection against direct rifle fire, but in modern warfare, the soldier's chances of escaping a direct hit are high. ■ Armor, a vital part of the equipment of today's fighting man, is not yet a relic of ancient history. More machine-pressed helmets have been produced in a few years in Detroit than handmade helmets in fifty centuries of military history. These workaday helmets and body armor cast no bronze gleam across a plain, nor do they light up the sky, but they have won the respect of their wearers and they can share in the glory of the helms and suits of armor once worn by kings and emperors, glistening with precious metals and glittering with jewels. Their dents and scars are the signs of men saved from injury and death.

INDEX

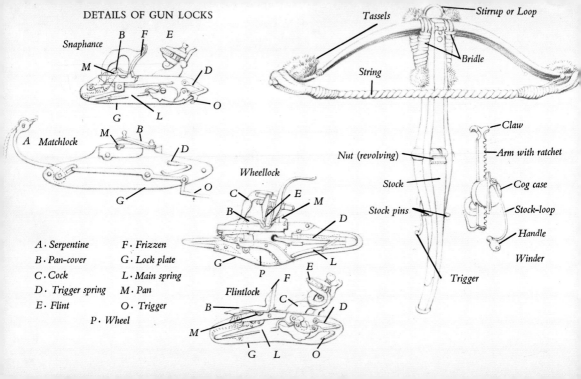

DETAILS OF GUN LOCKS

Snaphance

Matchlock

Wheellock

Flintlock

A · Serpentine
B · Pan-cover
C · Cock
D · Trigger spring
E · Flint
F · Frizzen
G · Lock plate
L · Main spring
M · Pan
O · Trigger
P · Wheel

Tassels

Stirrup or Loop

Bridle

String

Nut (revolving)

Stock

Stock pins

Trigger

Claw

Arm with ratchet

Cog case

Stock-loop

Handle

Winder